a spell for living
KEISHA-GAYE ANDERSON

For the oracles and the seers. Make these words your talisman.

A SPELL FOR LIVING

Copyright © 2020 by Keisha-Gaye Anderson
All rights reserved

Published by Agape Editions
http://agapeeditions.com
Binghamton, NY

The Morning House e-chapbook series is published by Agape Editions, in partnership with THEThe Poetry Blog. All Morning House titles are available from Agape Editions and THEThe Poetry Blog as free, downloadable e-books.

ISBN: 978-1-7364655-0-9

Editor: Jasmine An
Assistant Editor: Fox Henry Frazier
Cover and Interior Art: Keisha-Gaye Anderson
Cover and Interior Design: Cristina Castro Pelka

Music by SmartBlackKid
https://soundcloud.com/keisha-gaye-anderson

Library of Congress Control Number: 2021935872

Some of the poems in this collection have appeared in the following publications: *Interviewing the Caribbean, African Voices Magazine, The Killens Review of Arts and Letters, The Mom Egg Review: Vox Mom, Poetry in Performance* (2016), *Soul Sister Revue* (Jamii, 2019), *Multilingual Anthology: The Americas Poetry Festival of New York* (Artpoetica, 2014), *Culture Push,* and Split This Rock blog.

CONTENTS

Invocation 2
Unravel 4
The World 6
Stay Awake 8
Dis/Ease 10
The Day After: 2016 Presidential Election 12
The Purge 14
Subsistence Life 16
Classism 20
Spin 22
For Freddie Gray and All Those Murdered by State Violence 27
Remote Control 31
Fly 34
What I Know 36
I Move 38
We Talawah 39
Time is a Suggestion 40
Time is Tangled 43
A Spell for Living 48
To Artists 51
A Message to my Descendants 52
Black Is Not Enough 55
We Are a Star 58
Music of the Spheres 60
Tell Them 62
Be Fabulous 64

Invocation

Hey!

Aren't we them?

Those same ones
who spoke shapes
into the mist
and birthed ourselves
on the other side
of forgetting
so we could become
a soaring
spiral of stardust

Wasn't it us
who gave the blues
a language
and drummed escape routes
into maps while we were at it?

Isn't this me and you
the same them from
back then who carved
equations into stone
so we could reassemble our thrones
when the world
would make our amnesia
its national pastime,
economic plan,
and sexual obsession?

Yes.

You are the answer
to your own question

Now, get to work.

Unravel

I came here
just to unravel
your illusion
throw red paint/saint words
in this space

Watch:
My waist
and hips be
cymbals
pulling waves
in their wake

My hair
free like
yam vine
breadfruit tree
be persistent
dissonance

A steamy wet tango
in a ballroom
a bare brown ass
in a courtroom

I mean, we all split
in the middle
the same way

Which way galaxies
collide
explode into awareness

How come you so blind
and careless?

No,
this just won't do

The eyes are a liar
there's more than
sinew in you
is me
is us
is one very old
idea

But if you insist
on being the very least
the willfully blind
and skillfully weak
then I will have to bounce you
with my big body
Mami's temple
template for a people
and let my electric fire
jump start your heart

How could anyone who
truly feels love
be merely the sum
of their parts?

The World

I want to tell you the world is fair,
baby love
that we, like streams and saplings,
move in perfect time
to the cycles that push everything up
and out
turn these bodies into sun and rain
make our comings and goings
flow as seamlessly as the river's and ocean's
endless bachata

But there's a knot in the grid
a blindness that gridlocks
the mind
a mindless consumption
that locks down sight
a midnight of the spirit
that pushes us
through a maze
of clapboard and rust
a dust devil of fear that
resets the day
each time we start to see dawn
behind our eyes

Now, I don't want to lie to you,
sugar plum,
but the world is nothing
like you think
it is

And you can't ever get out
until you learn to see inside
out

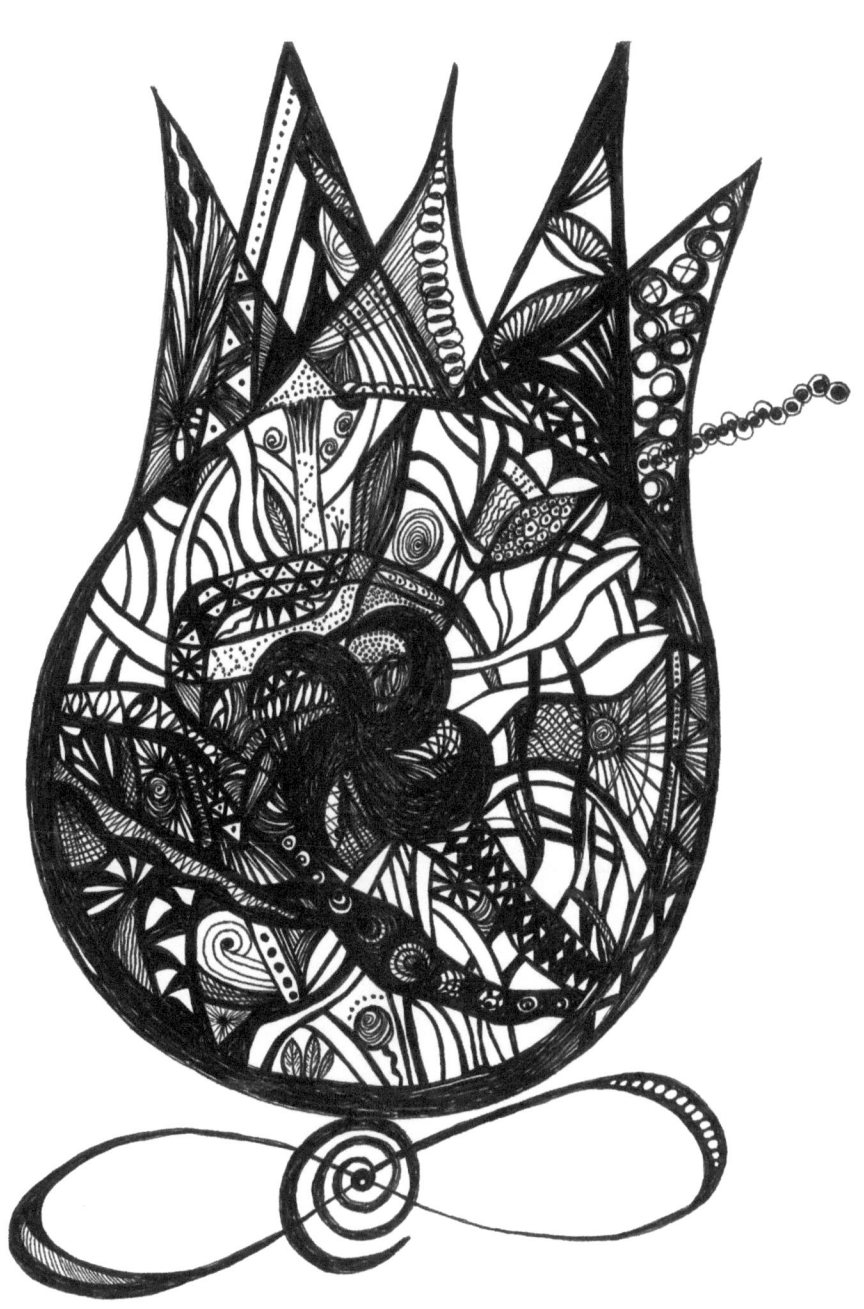

Stay Awake

Poor dear

You followed
a firefly question
down a ditch
into the dark
looking for a truth
a way to untangle
a why
stampeding through time
an avalanche of poison
turning all your names
to ash

And you landed
in a world of illusion
solidity cemented
by collective confusion
and the noisy madness
of breathing bodies
stacking bricks
to hoard life

All the plants
the rivers
the clouds gliding by
are the same swirling
song

A dream we play
and forget
that we are weaving
from the inside

Out of solutions
for seeing
our own faces
we keep chasing a tale

And forget
that we should
just laugh
at the shape of it
all

Follow the doors
to the end of the
maze

Stay awake
long enough
never to fall
again

Dis/Ease

Every time I see
a mad man
with his
dutty bungle
shuffling through
the tunnels veining
this grid
I think,
someone pushed him
through her flesh
into the world
didn't sit on his neck
loved him long enough
for him to not die

And then what happened?

When do all the doors close
on an unwell mind?

The Day After:
2016 PRESIDENTIAL ELECTION

After this day
you will not make
a fetish
of what you call my
"poverty"—
the stable you built
for me
to walk in circles
servicing machines
that push food down
your bottomless gullet

We are done dancing
on your stage
we will no longer compress
the fire of our stars,
netted in flight,
diverted down into dirt,
to illuminate
the cave
that is your mind

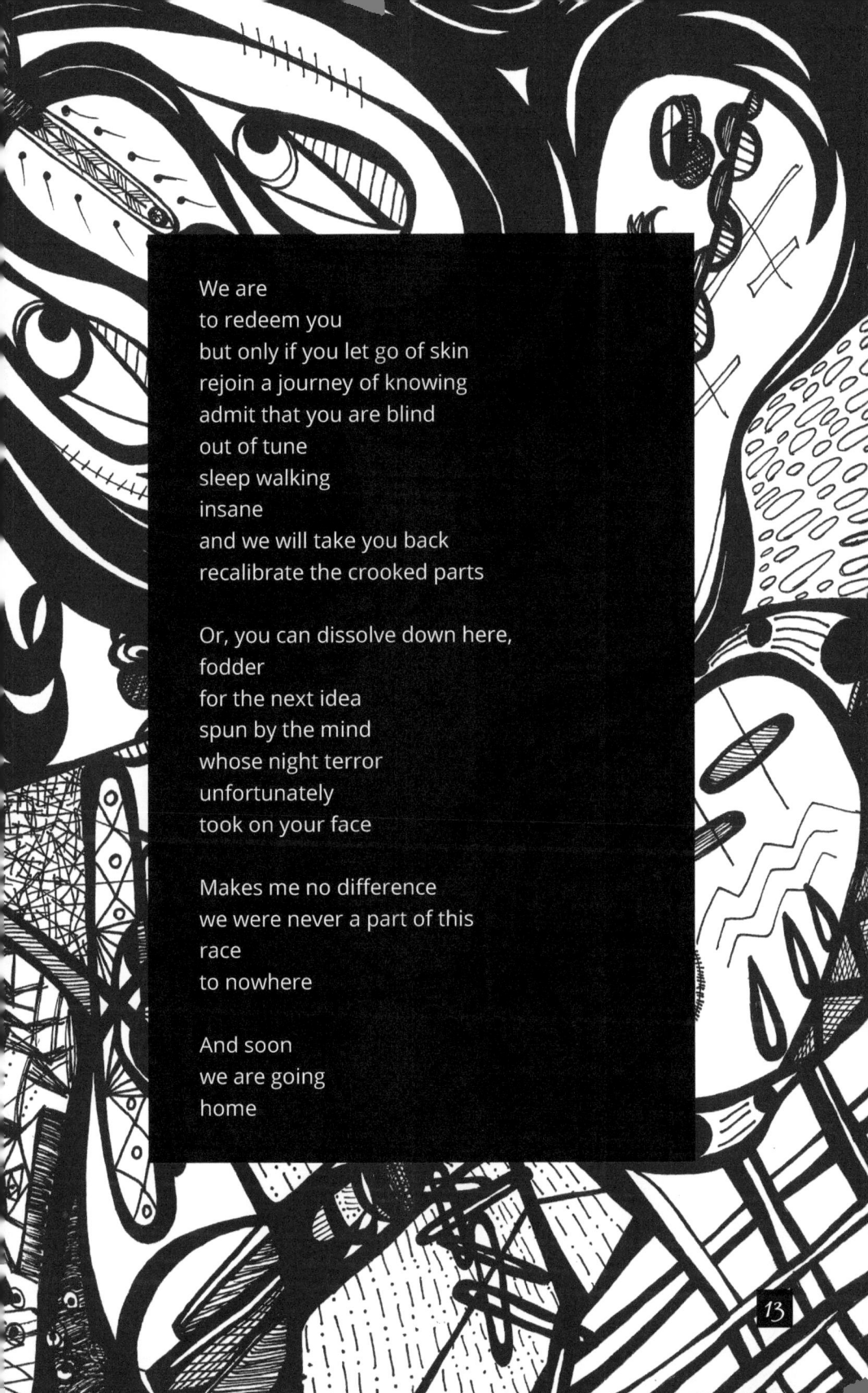

We are
to redeem you
but only if you let go of skin
rejoin a journey of knowing
admit that you are blind
out of tune
sleep walking
insane
and we will take you back
recalibrate the crooked parts

Or, you can dissolve down here,
fodder
for the next idea
spun by the mind
whose night terror
unfortunately
took on your face

Makes me no difference
we were never a part of this
race
to nowhere

And soon
we are going
home

The Purge

Fools believe
we are only
space warmers
place sitters
hewers of wood
diggers
builders
for their benefit
for those who inherit
empire
commit urban renewal
raise taxes
to purge the obstinate
depreciate any evidence
of your sweat
as you climb up
the down escalator
of manufactured debt
and end up sleeping in a cardboard box
holding court with the last
threads of your mind

And if you're not one of them
well, you'd better sing and dance
so that they don't devour your babies
appropriate the life right out of you
collect your organs
just to "see"
(file that under Tuskegee)

And how did they happen?

I mean,
what's the cause behind a
disease?
A crooked thought
splitting into
interlocking cubes
stacking themselves
into a sprawl
a bundle of cells
thinking itself sentient
reproducing
without bearing
right toward
light
into something
useful
turning life into ash
and dressing death
as a marionette

When cities are erected
everywhere
what
of us
will be left?

Subsistence Life

This subsistence life
thick with lonely universes
spinning themselves out
on stages
built of their own cravings
with scarce a nerve left in them
to feel each other's rotation
in these movements that create
somethings
full of no thing
each generation

I want us to collide
Big   and   Bang
explode a wake
raze the dead
in this matter
suffocate shallow chatter
led by money
and other
fictions

I want us to unveil
the real
then disappear
through the center
of the clock
the shape of our
racetrack

I will
we never look back
demolish the circle of lies
that shanty around our hubris
cement stacks
of convenient hallucinations
to chain us to this ladder
sinking into
mud
when pressure
meets each
rung

I see us collapsing
the loop
going deep inside
becoming one mind
one sound
single vantage

Burn the buildings they bury
us under
any time we wonder
what voice is yelling
"Wake up!"

I have no hunger
to see
what's next

I want
us
right now
one sound
deep drum
more living
than heartbeat
the frequency
before it splintered
into language
mammal
and gender

Fly away from the madness,
plug into
us selves
let the cannibals
be

You can't teach them to see

Classism

Classism is a defunct
course of study
the self has a blueprint
that creates one mind
the time we spend
splintering into
multitudes
is a circle
spinning so fast
we cannot see
all us selves

The same human   Just you
with the same ideas   me
the same family   us
same dreams   we
same desire to know   am
what is
what next   How foolish is
where is evermore   man

They slice us up
live in layers
count us out
divide
calculate the volume
remains the same
the insane love fractions
counting parts
is as useless as drawing a line
in water

There is no other

Spin

The high science
of organized
distraction
called media
state policy
best practices
the oldest con game going
glass half empty
numbing of your knowing

You know,

I bet we could even
remember how to fly
if there were no 24-hour news cycles
reminding us to muzzle
the very song
that brought us here
through sweet waters
into heartbeat
arms and eyes
searching the sun
for some memory of
the trip
into this
abyss

And even amidst
the sunken islands
of your memory
that guard that road map
for you
for later
for when you grow up
and out of this skin,
you still enjoy
the stampede of spring colors
the sunset pirouettes
of starlings
and your lover's
salt/warm lips
whispering the way
to bring more people
to this party

But the spin wants everything
you're made of
will keep your teeth
in its Mississippi pantry
consume you like a

hyena hauling an antelope
from a watering hole that has
dried up

The fights they choreograph
are wearing your face
and you are accused
fit the description
have no identification
are illegal
are a lethal spark
that must be neutralized
before the cane field is ash
before the banks crash

But baby,
we are trick candles
Didn't you know that?
They can never put us out

We've just got to

Stop

Halt the rotation
of lies
this spiral of
absurdities

We are more than
eyes
ears
eating mouths
warm bodies
walking the Earth
consumers

We are
goddamn
mothafuckin
magic

Know this.

Come together
now

It's time

For Freddie Gray
AND ALL THOSE MURDERED BY STATE VIOLENCE

Me...
Mine...
My...

What?

You will all expire
whether your spine
is crushed
in nine places
or your body just
runs out of breath

And right after
your death
some other
voice talking through dirt
shaped into skin
will walk
on electric
currents
to the timer ticking down
the days
while singing the same damn song
you did

A solo called ego
composed in a state
of amnesia

And then what?

Grass will still grow

snow will still fall
life will still turn itself inside out
through the mouths of
every creature
formed from a similar equation
to yours

Why not move something?
Why not change the melody?

Tune the voices
to the thrashing branches
bowing in March breeze
train them to sing
like the dots of green
bravely stretching skyward
into the unknown

There is nothing to own
there is only to see
and to understand
why you came
that there are others here
and they are your air
you are their water

God is not
'out there'
but everywhere
in each other

Remote Control

No body
no more
wants to
hear words
that condense
in their own minds

These times
spin us like tops
and we whirl
on cue
toward spaces
that deal the daily dose

Mirages of hope
duplicated
on cotton notes
fuel organized confusion
that burrows into our seams
and bite by bite
book ends our dreams

It seems
we can't shake loose
the noose
hanging on
the hinges of this state
that echo locates you
wherever you be
and creates things like races
as it serves their needs

But if you only knew
the sky is blue because you
imagined it that way
once, before time was real
and that your very body
is a song hummed by God

You would wake up
open the windows of your temple
and have real church

You would acknowledge that
the costume of your countenance
is just dirt
like everything else on this earth
and you would plant ideas
in fertile grounding
reshaping what was cracked
by the silencing of drums
and fear of the dark

You would know that
your thoughts are
a dream
dreaming itself
into solidity
and death is just
dismissal from grade school

You would straighten
your backs so that
the idlers have nowhere to sit

And you would come back to
You
move with purpose
dance a new existence
into life
through resistance
all the while knowing
that you are the first smile
of the eternal Soul

We can't go home
living on remote control

Fly

How can there be a victor
when all of life
is an insatiable
mouth
eating its way around
a circle
you can't see?

The eaten will
eat the eater
in every combination
for which there are
numbers
like the fourth book
the laws of a god
the cube it constructed
the bloody finite
built of banality
and bewilderment

No.

I want to fly
outside of predation
where time is a memory
and the fire
that moves these legs forward
is itself
just for the sake of it
no longer needing to
push a horse
of bone and amnesia
a desperate opinion
longing to be heard
a hard return
disconnect

that moves
through cycles of want
that can never be satisfied

Where do the rivers end?
Is the food chain not a
sphere?
You know that you are
but do you know where is
here?

No.

I want to see through
every window of my soul
and remember
the gunfire
and cries of motherless
children
the rage of children
who should be men
the senselessness of
sentience
in a barbed wire cage
where sugar and sleep
are solace
as solely a bad dream
a night terror
a road I never have to walk
again

What I Know

My people,
I don't know what to tell you
when the guru says
your stress ain't situational
that your sugar is just hereditary
and cancer is the family
disease

Or when the baba makes you
send birds into the breeze
with your bilious trauma
whispered into their wings

I just know that I love you

And that you are the beginning and end of all beauty

I just know that the world broke you
and scattered the salt of your suffering in four directions
but the drum is calling us back together

I just know that the upside down tries to detonate you
when you reach to flip the hourglass
but the creator has a stopwatch
that can suspend every speck of dust

Mother is calling us

Stand sure
and know
the door is coming

I Move

I move
in this body
by the compass of my heart,
steeled for the fury
awaiting the waking
of the willfully dead
with my voice,
an echo in infinity,
in tune with the
chorus of existence,
harmonic resistance to
organized confusion
and collusion with
spirits lost in flesh.
What's left when
you burn away the fog
of deception?
A primordial fear
buckling under the weight
of its reflection.
Who will we be,
what will it teach us,
when we discover
who we really are?

We Talawah

We talawah,
Jamaica
spirits on a sojourn
through cracked drums
manacles
and scurvy faces

Meeting guardian
caciques in the land of Mami's
sweet water

And she organize
us all
by heart,
not by skin

We take
masks of race
and fling them up like
confetti
mix them up
like rice and peas

We melt
borders
with our bodies
to show you
One Love
all the currents
colliding
to light up
the mind like
lightning

This kind of unity
this kind of love
is the only reality
the world is
fighting

Time is a Suggestion

Children know that time is a suggestion
a trampoline where they
leap into the shape
of imagination
without fear of falling
or breaking in two

But what happened to me
and you?

We wear the years like badges
or barnacles
reeking of lessons without logic
or expiry
and sometimes,
in some minds,
the time is a tangle of vines
that constrict
a vice grip
of guilt
of possibilities pulled down
in mid-flight
and we suffocate under our own
weight

But if we only could remember that
time is a suggestion
we would recognize the question
that built this body
and become light

Make this Earth trip
into a party
not a fight

Time is Tangled

There is no time in heaven,
you know
Time is tangled
stitched through earth
holding us all
like mother holding a dirty diaper
My grandmother saw sprits
they didn't believe her
I dream what's coming
they suck their teeth
And say quietly,
"Tell me…"
Life is simultaneous
lifeissimultaneous
everywhere at once
Physical worlds
life times
fingers in the pond of the visible
There is the main percussion
and an off beat
in reggae
they swing on each other through the air
create a loud silence
a space that cradles close bodies
a vortex

Time is not real
my daughter was my mother
my son was my son
I lived in Alexandria
and I burned alive
next to books
I am still burning
still collecting words
and piecing together a map
to where?
Humans are like the tentacles
of an octopus
all moving separately
all connected
We can't go to heaven
until we all go to heaven
We can't go to heaven
until we are all loving
I'm tired of coming here
Where did King Leopold go?
He must be back here multiplied
multiple lies
lying babies in coffins
motherless daughters
My daughter clings to me
like we are supposed to be one person
the cat clings to me
like we are supposed to be one entity
Separation is pain
we are supposed to be one...

One what?
I am Keisha today
and don't you forget it
How do flowers know to grow?
What is our name?
When can we go home?

A Spell for Living

Crumple up your
birth certificate
toss it in the trash
set ablaze dollar bills
and fashion a picture
with the ash
a doorway
that pulls through
the dreamer
dreaming you
and let her
spend the day
naked in bed
then storm the church
and use the holy water
to douse your head
kick over the lectern
and slide between
the pews
write the names
of all your lovers
on Pomba Gira's shoes
greet her with champagne
that you let drip
over your tits
drenching the altar
where every
shape of you sits
atop white lace
underneath candle glow
where she touches them
to see through

the retina of you
work you like a
crochet needle
flood you with
whispered words
and images that say:
Waste no more time
running this race
that you started in your sleep
fuck respectability
become a thief
take back
your sight
flip reality upside
down
life is right behind
the curtain
that holds you to the
ground
seals you in skin
makes circles
of your
life
repeating
repetition
smothering
desire
before you leave
this desert
set yourself on fire

To Artists

Take the puzzle pieces and make a placard,
a sign that shows us how
one piece
is the whole part
how one heart
is us all beating
as a drum
finding ways through
the lies
written in the fine print
of every fake cause
requiring your blood
on the dotted line

And make us really see
this life

When you sculpt your reality in verse
and paint
and clay
show us
that all we've been doing
is staring into the dirt
and scratching our heads
trying to understand
why generations keep walking
in circles
when WE are the eye
of the storm
the spark
in the big machine

And we can cut off
the engine any time we are ready
but we need the lantern
of your vision
to stay steady

A Message to My Descendants

No matter
when you're born
you will be whipped
in the sandstorm
of seismic colonies
colliding by their dividing
and parching the earth
to bury life
denying any evidence
of our presence

And there is nothing to do
but endure it
because this world will always be
two halves
of the same misery
even when pleasure is the center
of your breathless desires
the axe of duality
is swinging back
to sever your head

But as I said before:
We don't dwell here

We will never do well here
in this colosseum
of the ravenous blind
whose destiny it is
to devour

We must fly above the hours,
my children,
bring our
two halves
into one focus
or risk riding this train
forever

It is madness to walk
on two feet
divide your days
according to
digestion

We are more than this encasing
we are the breathing
question
the intelligence
that renders
mother's hemline
draped across the cosmos
the stars in her gown
reminders of the sea
where we sleep
and just like her
we can flash our skirts
and vanish
when we feel to be
free

I promise you
Earth is not your home

it is only the testing ground
the tempering space
a place to wield your
wisdom
wrestle truth from fiction
fight for your every eye
to see

But after that,
let the dead
lay with the
dead

Fly home
to me

Black Is Not Enough

Black
is not enough
to go by
is too narrow
a space
too clumsy a way
to reveal
you

Don't you see
your place
up high
along the winding trail
of lights
resting on
Mother's neck?

Can you name
all the shapes
of your intelligence,
that sometimes,
when it feels like,
splashes over the brim
of infinity
to condense as jazz
a dance of colors
at 5Pointz
Denzel's deep-sea eyes
and our snaking hips
to the dancehall riddim's
dip
dip dip
dip
dip dip
dip—

Unleash your
ecstatic laughter
for this joyous walk
through time
and mirrors
where you can love you
as us,
as all of this
salt foam under a lavender sun
the jubilant tail
of your familiar
a warm kiss of wind
in a glade
exploding with new life
that sweet sacrifice
of guiding
the next navigator
of your blood

Black is not enough
is too dim an idea
too minuscule
a name
for us

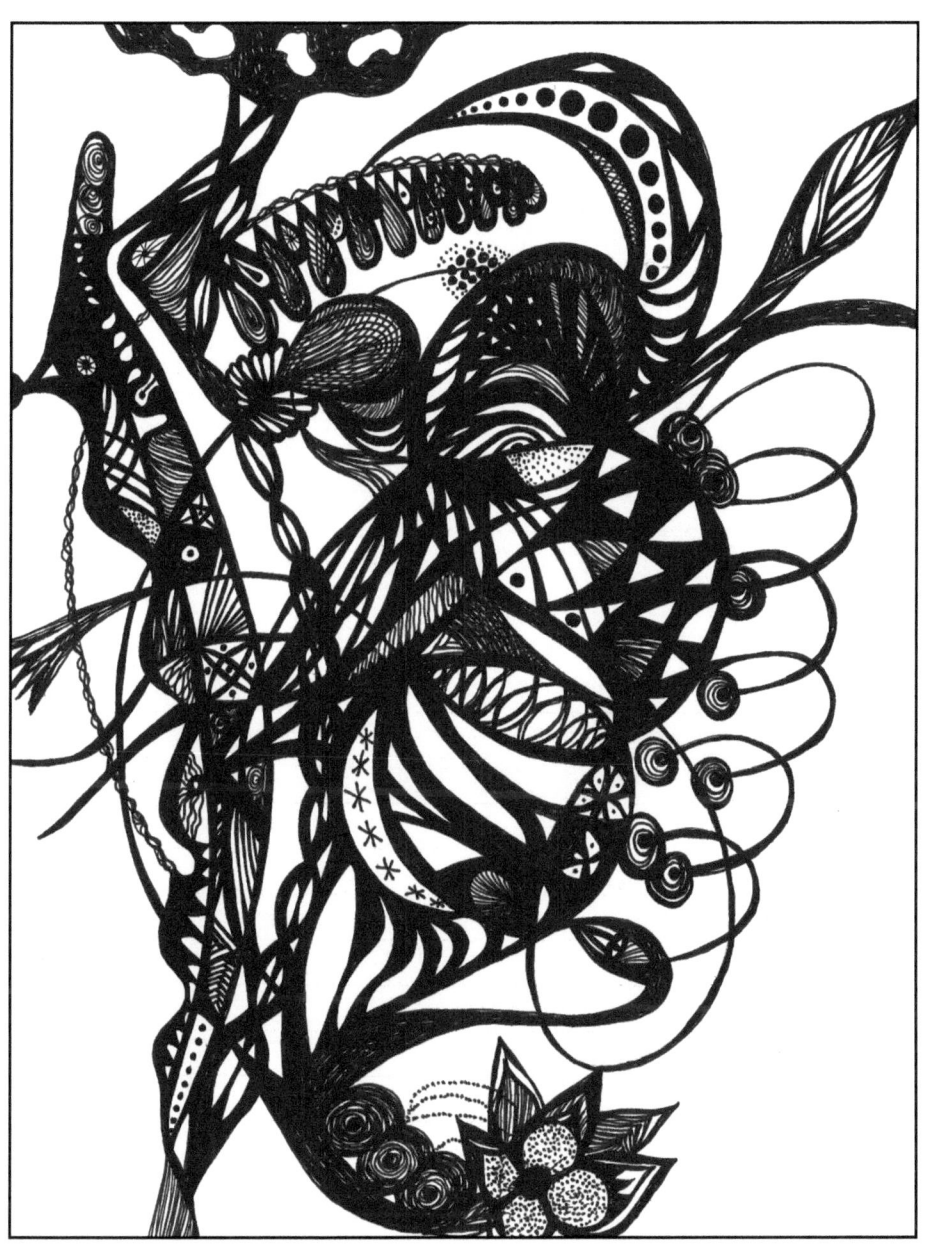

We Are a Star

Baby,
we are a Star—
all of us

But if you want to know
what makes this point
of light
pierce the dark,
I have to unfold
the scrolls of our existence
and show you many lives,
package them in gender,
lovers' eyes,
epistles written in laughter,
statues curved like desire,
perfume named loving
resting in floorboards
and the mirror of time

Our faces are a chain link
a latticework of memories
stretched out from my sleeping mind
like wings
across midnight

We are a red carpet unfurling
the story written in blood/ink
that chants me into an epic
of flesh and movement
with each new question
we think

Ours is the map
riding on swirls of brisk air
whispered through slumber
from far
but near

We understand
to take this mission
walk toward tomorrow
pull the world with us
lift the voices arrested
in hungry throats
bend the corners
back into a circle
as we move
up
up
up

to meet ourselves
with each revolution
so that each one
learns to fly
and finally realize
once again
the way to be
without end

Music of the Spheres

The point is
just
to sing together

Uni/verse
one song
simple notes
that stitch you
seamlessly into
the finest temple
bars humming your
question
through the light of your eyes
percussion pulsating
stars into sky
also keeping time
in your chest

And all there is to do
is step to that song
be a ripple
in the wave
that must wash
the Earth
dissolve the circle of
birth
death
forgetfulness
that swirls
around you
and rest yourself
in the center

Yet, here we are
again
searching for the magic
words at dawn
after dreaming in the melody
all night

This time is always
perfect
is just for
play
and dancing
together
to remember
what we already know

Breathe in tune
to the music of the spheres
and slip your selves out of these
bones
exhale with Mami

Come home

Tell Them

Tell them I was a big woman
tall and unyielding
who lived out loud
unmoved
in front of
the blurry chaos
of the city

Tell them I was the eye
whipping the wind
around me
as I walked through
the places
of learned insanity

Tell them I was every deluge
that ever stopped traffic
laughing as they spun their wheels

Tell them I was the red clay
that demanded intelligent seeds
to grow nourishing questions
and fruitful answers

Tell them I was as kinky
and cloistered as my curls
and only deep water
free divers
could reach my door

Tell them I was all that
and much more
they couldn't see

Tell them
they could never really know
me

Be Fabulous

I mean,
stand up and say
I am
without words
know that
you are moonlight
pushing aside the night
a hearth warming
chests into a wave of motion
when grief slowly siphons breath

No need to scream about
what is not
or lament
the crazy
of they—
the oldest tale
of hungry chasing its tail
We are older than all that
before the buying
and selling

Reluctant or not,
we are creators of culture
purveyors of cool
distilled diamonds
ditching the dirt
of a thousand long marches
through manacles
cane and cotton
assembly lines
back doors only
first-name nannies
wet nurses whose own children

rocked with rickets
medical guinea pigs
men who are always boys
who are made the blame
for a leaky economy built like a sieve
in seismic ground

We been around long enough
to know
that no man
put salt in the ocean
and that Nat Turner
was speaking to God himself
as himself
and then made those two selves
agree to proceed
with an overdue lesson

We are to lead
even reluctantly
because time breathes in
and out
on a scale the mind
can't measure
but which the soul sees
and plots a journey
of light
sound
color
vibration
a path up and out for those
trapped inside the smallness
of things
a gracious door of salvation
out of ignorance

Don't spend time
trying to convince me
or her or them
you're fabulous

Just BE
who you already
are

www.ingramcontent.com/pod-product-compliance
Lightning Source LLC
Chambersburg PA
CBHW042236090526
44589CB00006B/77